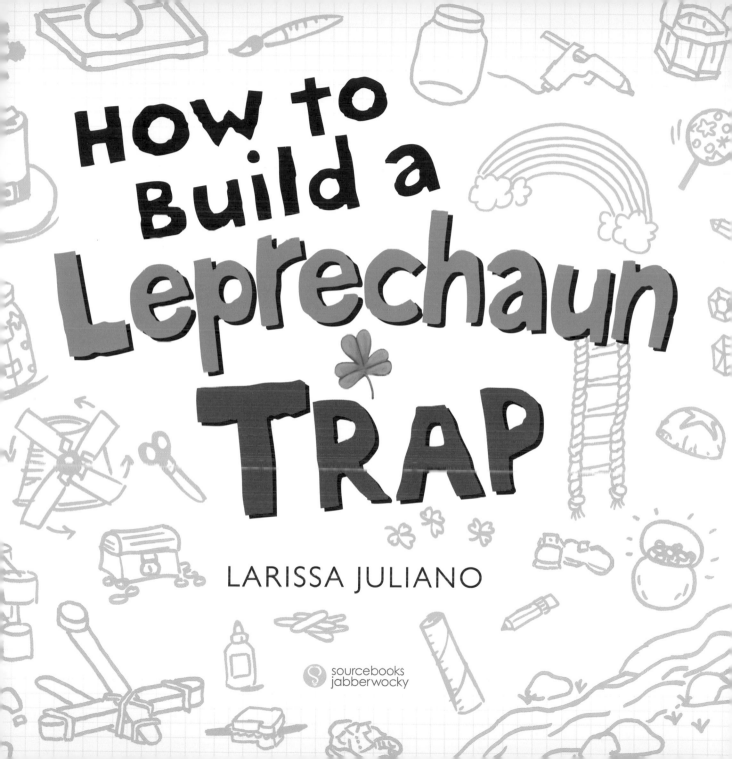

How to Build a Leprechaun TRAP

LARISSA JULIANO

sourcebooks
jabberwocky

Published by Sourcebooks Jabberwocky, Sourcebooks, Inc.
P.O. Box 4410, Naperville, Illinois 60567–4410
(630) 961–3900
Fax: (630) 961–2168
sourcebooks.com

Source of Production: Worzalla, Stevens Points, WI, USA
Date of Production: October 2017
Run Number: 5010793

Printed and bound in the United States of America.
WOZ 10 9 8 7 6 5 4 3 2 1

CONTENTS

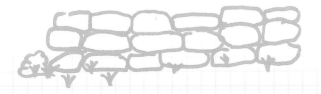

NOTE TO PARENTS

Doing hands-on projects with our kids can be one of the most engaging and fun ways to spend time together! With so much technology and screen time, getting kids to use their hands and imaginations is truly one of the best gifts we can provide. Children are naturally inquisitive about how things work. It's great for them to show interest, but it can feel overwhelming for parents trying to keep up with the latest trends and activities, all the while trying to stay present and engaged during these precious childhood years.

Engineering something as fun and quirky as a leprechaun trap gets children involved in the entire process, from thinking of clever ways to catch the sneaky little leprechaun to building the trap, creating a conversation and sense of accomplishment. These are the kinds of projects that families remember making together because everyone is able to contribute in some way. Whether it's planning the trap, reading the directions aloud, sketching the trap in a notebook, or constructing and decorating it, there really is a job for all.

This is why STEAM projects have grown in popularity and prevalence. STEAM stands for projects that include science, technology, engineering, arts, and mechanics. According to Engineering for Kids and the U.S. Department of Commerce, STEAM creates critical thinkers, increases science literacy, and enables the next generation of innovators.

Building a leprechaun trap is also the perfect STEAM challenge for families. Every trap in this book will incorporate the artistic component of using different art media and decorating, stylizing, and manipulating these materials. In addition, the STEAM connection box will specify what aspect of STEAM is being referenced—whether it's physics, engineering, math, science, or technology. Parents and children can use these teaching points to generate questions, have thoughtful discussions, and then decide how to take scientific inquiries to the next level.

Innovation is key, and the trap directions, fun facts, and STEAM connections should be a stepping-stone to the children's ideas and inquiries. The product of a leprechaun trap is awesome! But the process of creation is where the real magic happens. STEAM projects are meant to be open-ended with learning and discoveries unfolding as organically as possible, so encourage creative thinking even if it steers away from the directions. Collaboration, brainstorming, and inquiry are the heart and soul of STEAM projects, and developing these skills will go a long way for a child.

Note: Technology can be incorporated into each and every trap to inspire further research using digital and print resources at your local

library. Having a variety of resources at your fingertips allows kids to pull information, check for accuracy, and report their findings. Using the tablet or computer (with adult supervision, of course) is just another way to scaffold onto kids' knowledge and add to their existing schema of how things work. Remember, children often like to revisit ideas and creations over the course of several days. Leave your traps out to see what engineering enhancements they come up with.

STEAM TALK

As parents of our budding scientists and engineers, we also play the role of STEAM facilitator. Try your best to take a step back and allow your children to problem-solve and analyze the directions, and make modifications as needed. In addition to the STEAM connections to spark scientific dialogue, here are some other great open-ended questions/games to engage in during the leprechaun trap construction process.

- Describe how this trap works.
- Why do you think this is the best material for that step?
- Can you think of a better way to do this?
- Can you look at the picture and try to build the trap without the directions?
- Can you replace one of these materials with something else?
- What can you add to this trap?

INTRODUCTION

Have you ever wanted to catch a leprechaun? People have been trying to catch these sneaky Irish fairies for centuries! Often depicted as tiny elves dressed in green with buckled shoes and tall hats, leprechauns usually keep to themselves, mending shoes, hiding their pots of gold, and partaking in mischief toward human folk. According to legend, if they are caught, leprechauns will try to barter for their freedom by granting three wishes. But watch out—they are mischievous and clever little fellows who are known to cause trouble.

If you are up to the task, this book is a perfect place to start building, planning, and scheming. Not only do these traps satisfy the restlessness so many of us feel to manipulate, fidget, twirl, and cut, but they will make you and your family giggle and debate as you determine what little tricks and shiny gadgets may lure your leprechaun. Traps and projects range in complexity but can be easily modified to add more dimension and innovation.

Don't let this be the only book in your hands during this process! *How to Build a Leprechaun Trap* should be one of many resources on a journey with books and tools that engage, inspire, and motivate the whole family to use their gifts and ideas in innovative ways. Castle buffs? Check out the library to read about Ireland's rich history during medieval times. Foodies? Look up recipes together to include in your Shamrock Diner. Embracing and expanding your children's inquisitiveness will inspire them to discover topics they love.

This book is full of easy-to-follow instructions to build fifteen traps, with trivia about leprechauns and Ireland throughout. At the end of the book, there are a few planning pages to help you come up with your own trap and a set of stickers you can use to decorate these projects and lure in a leprechaun! In between the traps, there are additional activities and recipes to help get you in the leprechaun-catching mood. STEAM connections are at the beginning of every activity, which are meant to take learning further by looking at which part of STEAM plays a role in each project. These sections take a look at topics such as how gravity works to knock over our trap cup, the role that acceleration plays in our leprechaun marble run, and the types of energy that factor into these ingenious designs.

So now it's time to grab your glue gun and paint and start planning the perfect trap! Keep a look out for tiny footprints, sprinkles of glitter, or a trail of gold coins—leprechauns will not be able to resist sneaking a peek at (and maybe being caught in) your clever contraptions.

NOTE ON MATERIALS

Materials will be listed on each project page, but many can be interchanged depending on what you have on hand (and what inspires you in your creation process).

- Almost every trap will need some type of paint, markers, or crayons; glue; tape; and construction paper, so always have those materials handy.
- Clay, putty, or play dough can all be used as a sticky base to affix signs or other trinkets you would like to stay put.
- Hot glue works best for attaching most objects, but glue sticks or white craft glue can also be used.
- You can purchase colored craft sticks, or you can paint or color them yourself.
- For traps that require greenery, go in your backyard, or find faux moss and grass from your local dollar store.
- Foam board and cardboard can be interchanged, but foam is a bit easier to cut.
- Be creative with how you decorate your trap! Paint, glitter pens, markers, construction paper, and stickers will add personality to your trap.
- Glitter is optional for all traps. For less mess, substitute with sparkly wrapping paper, glittery scrapbook paper, glitter glue, or shiny paint, or create your own sparkly landscape with colored pencils or crayons.

REMEMBER:

- Leprechauns love shiny things! Look around the house (and backyard) to find some trinkets and treasures you could use as bait for your sneaky little green fellow.
- Rainbows attract leprechauns because they are hoping for that pot of gold at the end. You can add rainbows in lots of fun and creative ways, like rainbow buttons, pom-poms, paint, beads, pipe cleaners, and more!
- Gold, gold, gold! Pots of gold are what keep leprechauns on the prowl...and susceptible to your traps! This is a necessary addition to any trap you create.
- Leprechauns are cobblers and love mending and tending to shoes. If you hear the sound of a little hammer, your leprechaun is surely close by! Perhaps keeping your trap near the shoe closet is a good way to lure them from their hiding spots.
- Some materials or tools may require the help of an adult. An asterisk (*) next to an item will denote this.

PADDY'S CRAFT BOX TRAP

This colorful box can hold all the treasures your leprechaun
will lead you to (after you catch him, of course!).

DIFFICULTY

LEPRECHAUN APPEAL

MATERIALS

60+ craft sticks
Nontoxic acrylic paint
Craft glue
Hot glue gun*
Gold coins, candy, or other treasure
Paintbrush

STEAM CONNECTION

This trap will get you thinking like an engineer as
you figure out how many sticks you are going to
need to create your box and which angle you'll
need to set the craft stick to prop up the top of
the box. Need an extra challenge? Experiment
with other shapes and build a treasure holder in
the shape of a pentagon, hexagon, or octagon.

I

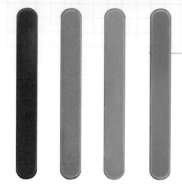

Painted craft sticks

1 Take forty craft sticks and paint them the colors of the rainbow. Let dry.

2 Overlap craft sticks to create a square. Dab glue in between layers. Layer squares on top of each other until you are out of craft sticks. If you want to make it taller, you can use more craft sticks to create more squares. Color combination doesn't matter—have fun with it!

Glue ten sticks across box to create a bottom.

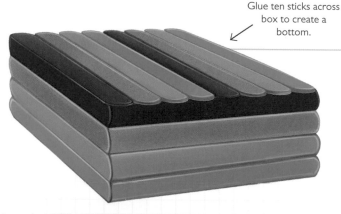

3 Take ten craft sticks, and with <u>adult supervision</u>, hot glue them across your square box. This will be the bottom of your box. Let dry.

Roof

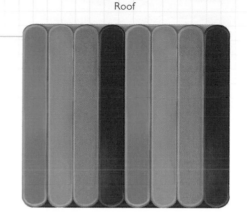

4 Flip over your box. Next, take two craft sticks and lay them parallel to each other. Dab glue to the edge of the sticks and add a row of ten sticks to create a top to your craft box.

Roof

Roof propped up by stick

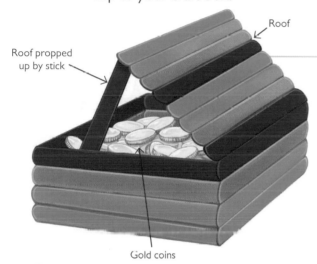

Gold coins

5 Find sparkly candy, gold coins, or marshmallow cereal, and sprinkle them on the bottom surface of your box. Prop up the lid with a final craft stick.

Be sure to let the glue dry! Your patience will pay off, as your leprechaun lad will surely be attracted to your rainbow hideout!

IRELAND   INDIANA

DID YOU KNOW?

The whole island of Ireland is about the same size as the state of Indiana. It takes less than eight hours to drive from the top of the country to the bottom!

SOMEWHERE OVER THE IRISH RAINBOW

Your leprechaun lad won't be able to resist this glittery
landscape of rainbows, sparkles, and crunchy treats!

DIFFICULTY

LEPRECHAUN APPEAL

MATERIALS

Hot glue gun*

Glue stick

Scissors*

Shoebox lid

Glitter construction paper, variety of colors

Cotton balls

Marshmallow cereal

Craft stick (or other device to prop up
shoebox lid)

STEAM CONNECTION

Time to put your engineering caps on! This trap
uses a craft stick to prop up the lid that will catch
our leprechaun, and it's up to you to figure out
which angle works best for the stick and lid.
Experiment with the angle of the stick and where
you position it against the lid to see which option
will hold up the longest and snatch the leprechaun
the quickest!

8½ x 11 in.
construction
paper

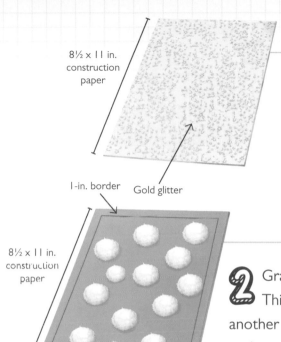

1-in. border   Gold glitter

8½ x 11 in.
construction
paper

Cotton balls

1 Glitter alert! Using a glue stick, spread glue all over the construction paper and sprinkle with gold glitter. Shake off excess. Let dry—this will be used for your cut-out gold coins later on!

2 Grab your glue stick again! This time, spread glue on another piece of paper and stick cotton balls all over it, leaving a 1-in. border.

3 Cut 5 x 1 in. strips of construction paper to create a rainbow path. Glue each colored strip to the top border of the cotton-ball paper.

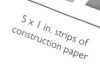

5 x 1 in. strips of
construction paper

5

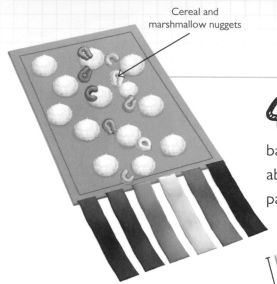

Cereal and marshmallow nuggets

4 Sprinkle marshmallow cereal nuggets on top of the cotton balls. (Your leprechaun won't be able to resist this rainbow-cloud path to sugary goodness!)

8½ x 11 in. glitter paper from step 1

5 Cut out coins from your glitter paper to add to your cloud in the next step.

Circles in shape of gold coins

DID YOU KNOW?

The weather conditions in Ireland are perfect for rainbows! This country sees so many rainbows because of the angle of the sun and all the rain that comes to the island. It's not uncommon to see two or three different rainbows in the sky all at once!

6 Wrap the shoebox lid in green paper (or paint it green). Prop up the lid with a craft stick (with its other end on the cotton-ball cloud) to create a *snappity snap trap* when your devious little fairy tries to eat his marshmallows!

Shoebox lid

Craft stick

SUPER-EASY IRISH SODA BREAD

A must-have recipe for your Shamrock Diner Trap. You will want this delicious soda bread every day of the year—not just St. Patrick's Day!

DIFFICULTY

LEPRECHAUN APPEAL

INGREDIENTS

4 cups white flour

4 tablespoons white sugar

1 teaspoon baking soda

1 tablespoon baking powder

½ teaspoon salt

½ cup (1 stick) butter, at room temperature

1 cup buttermilk

1 egg

½ cup raisins (optional)

For Basting

½ stick butter, melted

¼ cup buttermilk

STEAM CONNECTION

What happens when you bake bread? How do the ingredients work together to create something so delicious? Well, the yeast cells react with simple sugars. As the sugars are metabolized (cooked), carbon dioxide and alcohol are released into the dough, making the loaf of bread rise! Can you experiment with different types of flours? How does that affect the baking time? Are there other bread recipes you can look up and bake? Create a graph and invite friends over for a bread tasting party. Compare and contrast the texture, crust, sweetness, and ease of recipe.

1 With <u>adult supervision</u>, pre-heat oven to 375°F. Lightly grease a large baking sheet.

2 Grab your measuring cups and spoons. In a large bowl, mix together flour, sugar, baking soda, baking powder, salt, and butter.

3 Stir in 1 cup of buttermilk and egg (and raisins if desired).

4 Dust some flour on a cutting board or countertop. Grab your dough and knead gently on floured surface. Shape dough into a ball and place on a greased baking sheet.

5 In a small bowl, combine melted butter with ¼ cup buttermilk and brush top of loaf. Save the remainder of this mixture for basting (you will need to baste four more times).

6 With <u>adult supervision</u>, use a sharp knife to cut an X into the top of your bread.

7 Bake at 375°F until a toothpick inserted into the center of the loaf comes out clean, about 45 minutes (but check at the 30-minute mark and put aluminum foil on top if it's getting too brown). Baste your bread with the butter/buttermilk mixture every 10 minutes or so!

Makes great toast in the morning!

9

SHAMROCK DINER

Corned beef and cabbage—true Irish dishes—should definitely be on this diner's menu!

DIFFICULTY

LEPRECHAUN APPEAL

MATERIALS

Shoebox or box, small-to-medium size

Small utility knife*

Medium-size poster or foam board

Nontoxic acrylic paint

Paper plates

Decorations for window and door trim
(marshmallows, gemstones, etc.)

Craft sticks

Construction paper, variety of colors

Tissue paper, variety of colors

Clay or putty

Craft glue

Paintbrush

STEAM CONNECTION

Budding artists, engineers, and mathematicians will need to bring their keen eye and design skills to this trap. When constructing a building, blueprints are used to draw the layout. The blueprint was first created in the 19th century when architects wanted to reproduce drawings quickly since tracing the images took too long. To this day, architects, engineers, and shipwrights continue to use blueprints for their drawings. Sketching a blueprint of your own diner prior to cutting will allow you to visualize where you want your door and window frames (and other additions you might want to add!).

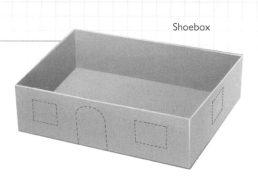
Shoebox

1 Cut out a door and several windows from your box.

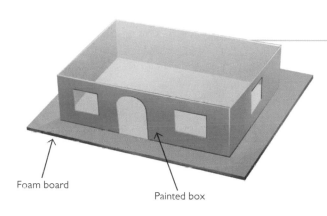

Foam board

Painted box

2 Paint box, or wrap it in green paper. Glue its bottom to a large piece of cardboard or foam board.

Paint

3 Cut paper plate in half. Cut a smaller half circle out on the bottom to create an arc, which will be used as a rainbow.

Paper plate

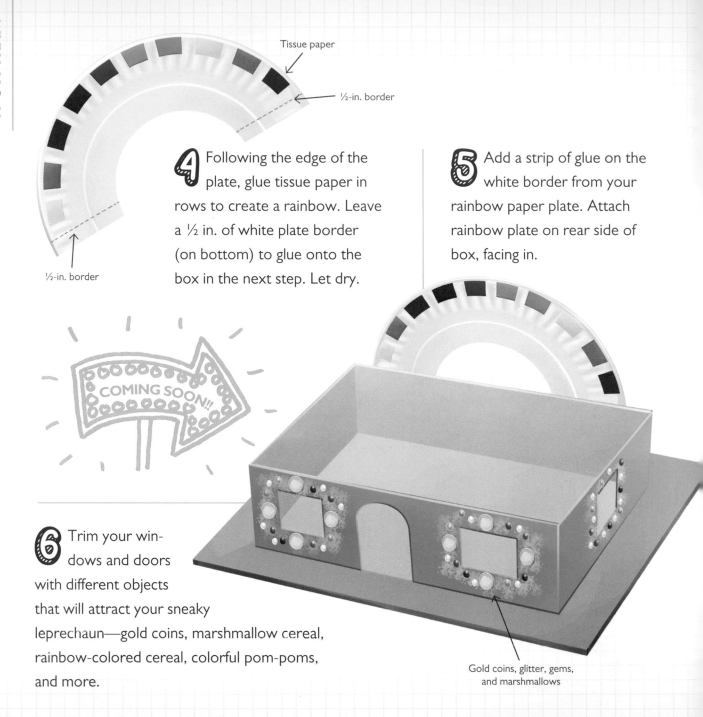

Tissue paper

½-in. border

½-in. border

4 Following the edge of the plate, glue tissue paper in rows to create a rainbow. Leave a ½ in. of white plate border (on bottom) to glue onto the box in the next step. Let dry.

5 Add a strip of glue on the white border from your rainbow paper plate. Attach rainbow plate on rear side of box, facing in.

COMING SOON!!

6 Trim your windows and doors with different objects that will attract your sneaky leprechaun—gold coins, marshmallow cereal, rainbow-colored cereal, colorful pom-poms, and more.

Gold coins, glitter, gems, and marshmallows

Paper

Craft stick in putty

7 Using a piece of foam or construction paper and craft sticks, create two signs for your diner—one for the name of your diner, and the other for some food items you think your leprechaun would like! Stick the base of your sticks in putty or clay to ensure they stay put.

8 Take your putty and shape a small flat circle to stick outside the door-way. Your leprechaun's pointy little feet will stick to this, and he will be trapped!

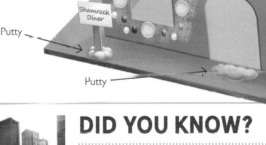

Putty

Putty

DID YOU KNOW?

Every year on St. Patrick's Day in Chicago, Illinois, the city dyes the Chicago River *green*! This tradition started in 1962 and continues to this day. Twenty-five pounds of special dye is used to turn about 1.5 miles of the river green. The color lasts for only a few hours.

13

SHAMROCK PRETZEL TREATS

Sweet and salty? Yes, please! These tasty shamrock morsels will delight the pickiest leprechaun trapper's taste buds.

DIFFICULTY

LEPRECHAUN APPEAL

INGREDIENTS

2 (10-oz) bags pretzels
1 (18-oz) bag green-coated candies
2 (13-oz) bags chocolate kisses
Baking sheet
Parchment paper

STEAM CONNECTION

In this activity, the chocolate is undergoing a phase transition as it goes from a solid to a liquid state—or, as it melts. When the chocolate is placed in the oven, the heat causes the molecules in the chocolate to move quicker than when at room temperature. This movement weakens the bonds between the molecules, which we see as the chocolate melts. Different chocolate melts at different temperatures, but it generally has a *melting point* (the temperature at which something goes from a solid to a liquid) between 86–90°F. Use different types of kisses to determine which chocolate melts the quickest!

1 With <u>adult supervision</u>, preheat oven to 350°F.

2 Line a baking sheet with parchment paper.

3 Spread pretzels out on baking sheet. Unwrap chocolate kisses and place one on each pretzel.

4 Pop your baking sheet in the oven for 5 to 6 minutes. When you remove the baking sheet, kisses will look intact, but they will be soft to the touch!

5 Gently press three green candies onto each kiss. *Work quickly—the chocolate will firm up, and it will be tricky to get your green candies to stick!*

6 Place the baking sheet into the freezer for 10 minutes to firm up your shamrock pretzel treats.

RAINBOW SPRINGS

Leprechauns might be stingy, but they still want to look good! Glittery goo is disguised as sparkly bath water in this irresistible trap.

DIFFICULTY

LEPRECHAUN APPEAL

MATERIALS

Construction paper, variety of colors

8½ x11 in. white paper, several sheets

Craft glue

Glitter

Shallow plastic dish

Lids to coffee cans, snack containers/tins, or small ice cream carton tops can work well too!

Cotton balls

Craft sticks

Clay or putty

Water

Writing utensil for sign

(such as a pen, pencil, or marker)

STEAM CONNECTION

For this trap, you need to think like a scientist and rely on your math skills. Experiment with the glue-water ratio to come up with a mixture that will be sticky enough to catch a leprechaun but clear enough to fool him! If there is more glue, will it still look like a bath? Will more water dilute the mixture and allow the leprechaun to escape?

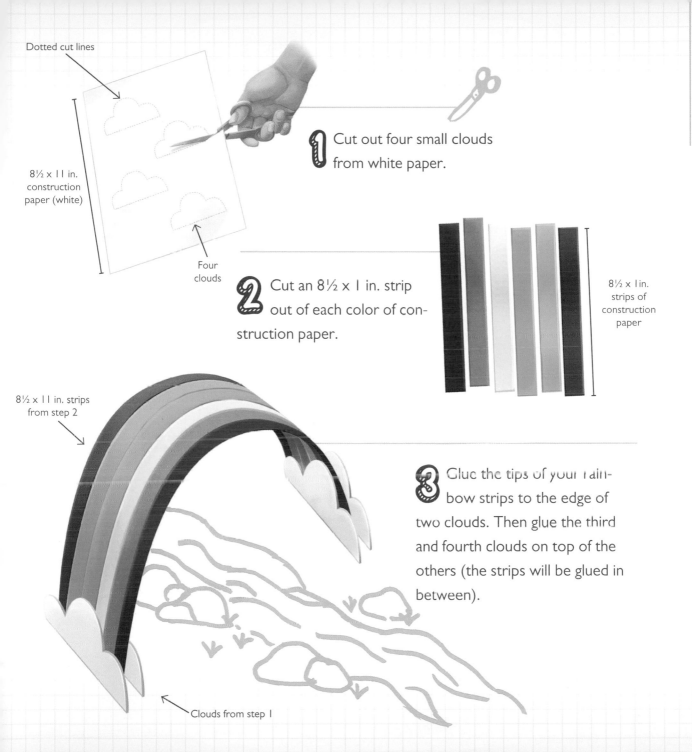

Dotted cut lines

8½ x 11 in. construction paper (white)

Four clouds

1 Cut out four small clouds from white paper.

2 Cut an 8½ x 1 in. strip out of each color of construction paper.

8½ x 1 in. strips of construction paper

8½ x 11 in. strips from step 2

3 Glue the tips of your rainbow strips to the edge of two clouds. Then glue the third and fourth clouds on top of the others (the strips will be glued in between).

Clouds from step 1

DID YOU KNOW?

Rainbows can be seen not just in rain but also in mist, spray, fog, and dew. If there is moisture in the air and light shining from behind at the right angle, a rainbow will surely appear!

(Above view)

4 Bend your strips into a rainbow shape, and glue the clouds at the base of an 8½ x 11 in. sheet of white paper.

8½ x 11 in. paper

5 Glue cotton balls around the perimeter of your paper.

Cotton balls

Glue

Water

Glitter

Shallow plastic dish

6 Time to make your glittery pond! In your small plastic dish, mix craft glue and water. Experiment with the glue-water ratio to get just the consistency you want. Sprinkle glitter over the mixture. Place this at the end of your rainbow bridge.

7 Add a sign using a craft stick and some clay for the base. The sign should tempt your little leprechaun into taking a bath in gold…only to get stuck in the glittery glue!

Piece of paper

Rainbow Springs

Craft stick

Putty →

WALKING RAINBOW

Can you make six colors of the rainbow using only blue,
yellow, and red? Try this experiment and find out.

DIFFICULTY 🍀

LEPRECHAUN APPEAL 🎩

MATERIALS

6 mason jars
Red, blue, and yellow food coloring
Paper towels
Water

STEAM CONNECTION

Color mixing and capillary action are at the center of this activity. What is capillary action? This is a process that occurs when water flows through the surface of other materials without the aid of any tools or manipulation—and this phenomenon is precisely what goes on in this activity. Vary the amount of water in the jars, mix colors, switch out cups, and use different kinds of paper toweling (does one-ply or two-ply paper allow the colors to travel faster?). Changing up *variables* (things that change in an experiment) can affect the outcome of your experiment!

1. Fill three jars with water.

2. Add several drops of red food coloring to one jar, blue to the second jar, and yellow food coloring to the third.

3. Form a circle with your six jars, alternating empty and colored jars.

4. Roll up paper towels into long cylinder shapes. Place one end of a cylinder into a full jar and the other end into the adjacent empty jar. *Repeat this step until each jar has two paper towel ends in it.*

5. Patience alert! This process will take about two days, but keep checking on it to watch the colors appear.

SHEEP PASTURE LEPRECHAUN SNATCHER TRAP

Nothing like a serene and lush pasture to attract your leprechaun's mischievous eye as he tiptoes near sheep and colorful windmills.

DIFFICULTY 🍀 🍀 🍀

LEPRECHAUN APPEAL

This trap will remind him of his beautiful Irish homeland!

MATERIALS

Hot glue gun*

Scissors*

Tape

Shoebox

Construction paper, variety of colors

Grass, twigs, and stones

Nontoxic acrylic paint

Cotton balls

Black pom-poms

Paintbrush

STEAM CONNECTION

This trap combines both science and engineering as you use the stick to prop up the box. Once the stick is knocked over, gravity will make the box fall, but will it be quick enough to catch your leprechaun? Engineering your trap accordingly will allow you to plan and prepare for your fast little fellow. Experiment with different stick lengths and see how much time it will take to fall (we hope!) onto your sneaky lad.

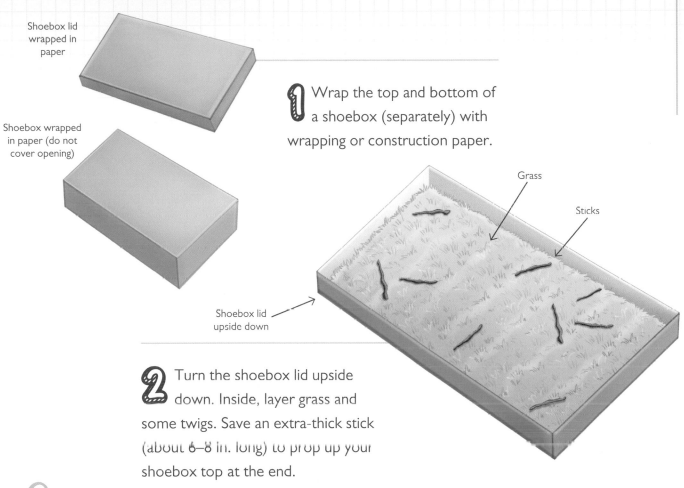

Shoebox lid wrapped in paper

Shoebox wrapped in paper (do not cover opening)

Grass

Sticks

Shoebox lid upside down

1 Wrap the top and bottom of a shoebox (separately) with wrapping or construction paper.

2 Turn the shoebox lid upside down. Inside, layer grass and some twigs. Save an extra-thick stick (about 6–8 in. long) to prop up your shoebox top at the end.

DID YOU KNOW?

There are more sheep than people in Ireland! According to the Irish Farmers Journal, the 2016 Ireland census found that there were 4.8 million people on the island and about 5.2 million sheep!

Paint

3 Paint some stones in gold, black, and white and lay them on top of the grass.

Stones

Black pom-poms

Cotton balls

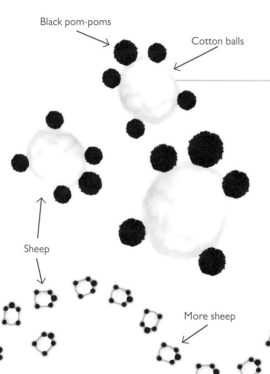

Sheep

4 Using a hot glue gun, glue black pom-poms onto cotton balls to create little sheep. Carefully cut pieces of cotton ball to stick onto the black pom-poms for the sheep's ears.

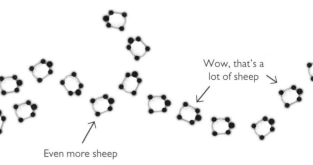

More sheep

Even more sheep

Wow, that's a lot of sheep

24

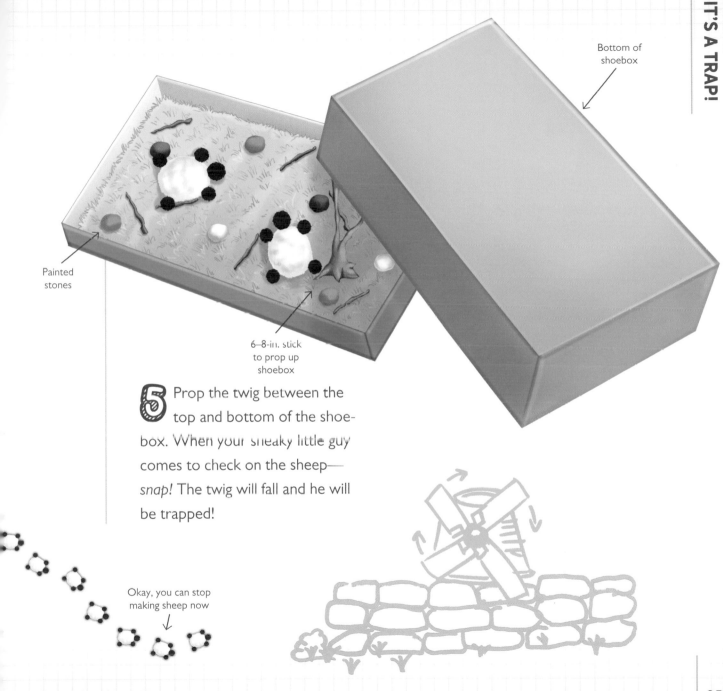

Bottom of
shoebox

Painted
stones

6–8-in. stick
to prop up
shoebox

5 Prop the twig between the top and bottom of the shoe-box. When your sneaky little guy comes to check on the sheep— *snap!* The twig will fall and he will be trapped!

Okay, you can stop
making sheep now
↓

MINI WINDMILLS

Create some mini windmills to make your sheep pasture look like authentic Irish farmland.

DIFFICULTY 🍀 🍀

LEPRECHAUN APPEAL

MATERIALS

Small paper cups

Scissors*

Nontoxic acrylic paint

Construction paper, variety of colors

Craft glue

1 brad

Small paper cup

Paint

1 Paint small paper cups. Let dry.

2 Cut out two fan blades from construction paper, about ½ x 2 in. Glue into a crisscross, one on top of the other.

8½ x 11 in. construction paper

½ in.

2 in.

½ x 2 in. strips of construction paper

3 Turn your cup upside down. Carefully poke a brad through the center of your crisscrossed fan blades and the cup, toward the top of the windmill.

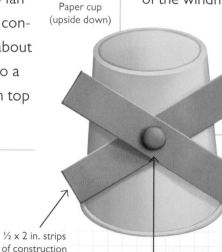

Paper cup (upside down)

Inside of cup

Sides of brad pushed down

Brad

4 Push down the sides of the brad inside the cup. Spin your fan blades around!

26

RAINBOW CHUTES AND LEPRECHAUN LADDERS

Who can resist a speedy slide? This delightfully fun trap will
bring out the fun in any grumpy leprechaun!

DIFFICULTY 🍀 🍀

LEPRECHAUN APPEAL

MATERIALS

Square tissue box (or similar style
　　box with opening on top)
Scissors*
Nontoxic acrylic paint
Craft glue
Hot glue gun*
Pack of drinking straws
Glitter
Paper towel tube
Cotton balls
Paper plate
Construction paper,
　　variety of colors
Crayons

STEAM CONNECTION

In this trap, you need your engineering
skills to create a ladder, making sure that
the side rails are tall enough to reach the
top of the box and that the rungs are
properly spaced. Did you know there
are two different types of ladders—rigid
and flexible? Rigid ladders are very sturdy
and come in many different forms, like
extension ladders, attic ladders, and fixed
ladders. Flexible ladders, such as a rope
ladder, are best used when storing
space is limited, but more skill is
needed to climb these ladders
because they tend to swing
like a pendulum. This trap
uses a rigid ladder, but how
could you change the design
and materials to create a
flexible ladder?

Flexible ladder

Rigid ladder

1 Paint the outside of the box green.

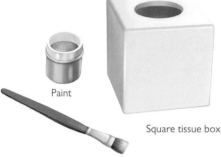

Paint

Square tissue box

2 Glitter alert! "Paint" your straw pieces with craft glue and sprinkle glitter on top. (You can also use markers instead of glitter.) Let dry.

Glitter-painted straws

Glitter

Glue

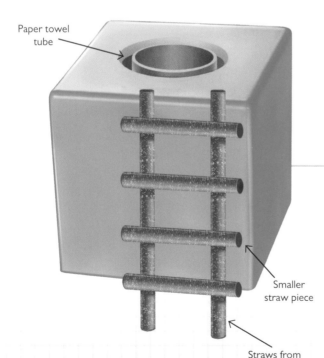

Paper towel tube

Smaller straw piece

Straws from step 2

3 Now make a ladder. With <u>adult supervision</u>, use a hot glue gun to attach two long straws (ladder rails) leading to the top of the box opening, and cut smaller straw pieces for the ladder rungs.

4 Take a paper towel tube and carefully cut it so it is the same height as the box. Hot glue the bottom of the tube and insert it into the box hole. Press gently to secure the bottom of the tube to the inside bottom of the box.

Paper plate

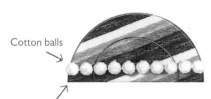

Cotton balls

Half of paper plate colored in rainbow colors

Crayons

5 Cut the paper plate in half. Color one half in rainbow colors; discard the other half. Glue some cotton-ball clouds to the perimeter of your paper-plate rainbow. Dab glue on the bottom of your paper-plate rainbow and attach it to the trap.

Note: Make sure it sticks out enough so your leprechaun can see it from the ladder.

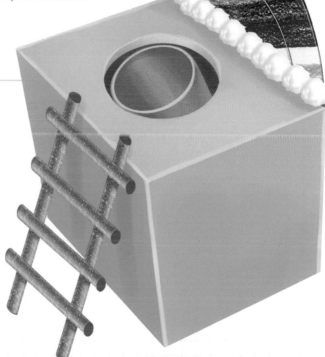

6 Take your construction paper and add some arrows and signs to direct your leprechaun up the ladder and down the chute!

DID YOU KNOW?
|||||||||||||||||||||||||||||||||||||||||||||||||||||

Centuries ago, leprechauns didn't wear green! According to Irish legends, they wore red jackets and red pointed hats.

ST. PADDY'S DAY DISCOVERY BOTTLE

Watching your glittery goo swirl around your bottle will help
you relax after a long day making tricky traps!

DIFFICULTY

LEPRECHAUN APPEAL

MATERIALS

Empty water bottle or other similar vessel

½ cup oil

Baby oil works best because it's clear.

½ cup water

Food coloring drops

1 (6-oz) jar of glitter

Small bag of green beads

Some pennies

Hot glue* or duct tape

STEAM CONNECTION

This activity shows how oil and water will never mix due to their different densities. Water contains many more molecules than water and therefore will always sink underneath the oil. If you shake your bottle the two liquids will emulsify, but then eventually separate again. The slickness of the oil allows your St. Patrick's Day objects to flow much slower through that jar versus a jar that just has water. A neat experiment is to try different ratios of water and oil, or water, oil, and dish soap. Dish soap has a different density than oil and water and generates a very interesting effect on the two liquids.

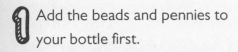 Add the beads and pennies to your bottle first.

Fill an empty water bottle half-way with baby oil.

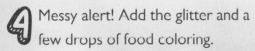 Pour water to fill up the rest of the bottle (leave a little room at the top to shake everything up!).

Messy alert! Add the glitter and a few drops of food coloring.

Secure the top of the bottle with hot glue or duct tape.

Shake your bottle and watch the magic happen! It is very relaxing to see how the glitter swirls and settles as you tip it back and forth.

The combination of oil and water can be used to create discovery bottles with any number of objects! Just be sure to secure the top.

IRISH CREAMERY

Sip on something sweet while you create this clever coffee concoction!

DIFFICULTY 🍀 🍀

LEPRECHAUN APPEAL

MATERIALS

Recycled coffee can

Scissors*

Green nontoxic acrylic paint

Small utility knife*

1 piece tissue paper

Hot glue gun*

Tape

Craft sticks

Decorations

Gold coins or mini pot
   of gold

String (optional)

STEAM CONNECTION

Using your engineering skills is a must for this coffee can trap. Figuring out how to glue the craft sticks perpendicularly and fastening the leprechaun bait requires careful planning, experimentation of different sized objects, and attachment tools. What else could you add to entice the leprechaun to the top of the can? Another ladder? More treats? Combine this trap with the Sheep Pasture to create a Leprechaun Trap Village.

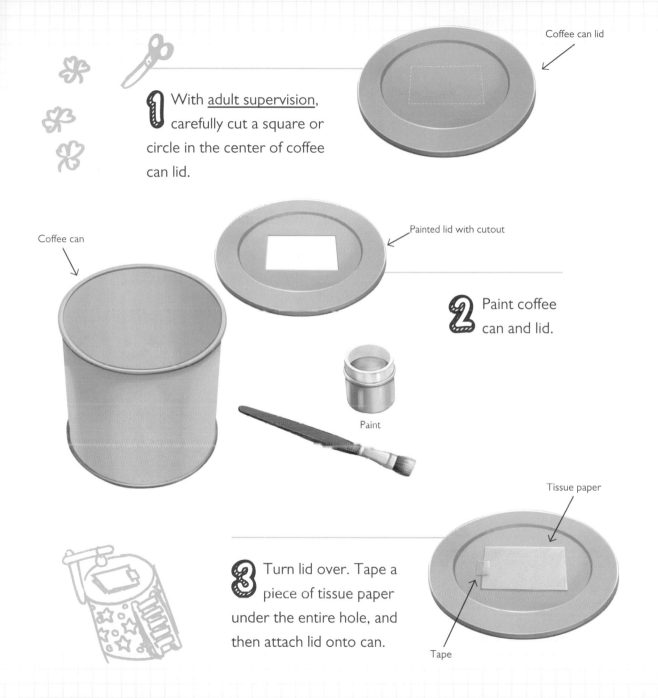

Coffee can lid

1 With <u>adult supervision</u>, carefully cut a square or circle in the center of coffee can lid.

Coffee can

Painted lid with cutout

2 Paint coffee can and lid.

Paint

Tissue paper

3 Turn lid over. Tape a piece of tissue paper under the entire hole, and then attach lid onto can.

Tape

33

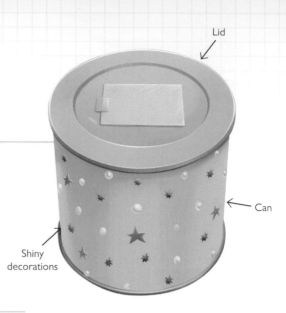

Lid

Can

Shiny decorations

Craft sticks

4 Time to decorate your can! Stickers are great for this activity.

5 Create a ladder by gluing craft sticks together for rails and rungs. Carefully cut sticks in half for the rungs if you do not want your ladder very wide.

6 Lean the top of the ladder on the edge of the coffee can (glue top rung to rim if necessary).

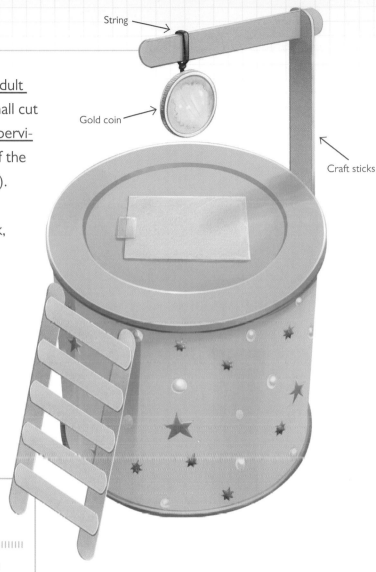

String

Gold coin

Craft sticks

7 Use a new craft stick and with <u>adult supervision</u>, carefully make a small cut at the top of the stick. With <u>adult supervision</u>, hot glue the stick to the edge of the coffee can (sticking up several inches). Grab another stick and slide the end through the small cut of the first stick, creating an upside down L figure. With <u>adult supervision</u>, secure with hot glue. The end of your perpendicular stick should be over the "secret" door covered with tissue paper. Attach a gold coin or mini pot of gold to the tip of your perpendicular craft stick (either with string or with hot glue).

DID YOU KNOW?

||||||||||||||||||||||||||||||||||||||||||||||||

Lucky charms include hanging a horseshoe above your doorway (U-shape—not ends down!), finding a coin or penny, and seeing a shooting star.

MARSHMALLOW CATAPULT

Watch out, leprechauns! Marshmallows are flying through the air with this clever contraption.

DIFFICULTY 🍀 🍀 🍀

LEPRECHAUN APPEAL

No leprechaun could resist shenanigans with a catapult!

MATERIALS

10 craft sticks

Bottle cap

4 rubber bands (have a few extra in case one snaps)

Mini marshmallows

Craft glue

STEAM CONNECTION

This catapult engages physics fans with potential and kinetic energy at its finest. When the craft sticks and rubber bands are pulled back, they have potential (stored up) energy, and when the bands are released, it creates kinetic energy (energy an object has in motion) that is transferred to the marshmallow, which is what sends the marshmallow soaring. Switch the mini marshmallow out for a larger one and see what happens to the distance that the marshmallow travels.

1 Take two craft sticks and stack them on top of each other. Fasten them together on one end with a rubber band.

2 Stack the remaining eight craft sticks and then attach together with a rubber band on each end.

3 Take your first two craft sticks. Carefully pull apart one end (rubber band attached on the other) and insert the stack of eight sticks.

4 The bottom stick will be the base of your catapult, and the top stick will be your launcher. Attach with the last rubber band, forming an X where the two craft sticks touch the larger stack.

5 Glue a bottle cap to the top craft stick, flat side down. Tuck your marshmallows into the open side before launching.

6 After the glue dries, try your catapult out! You can even make a target to see how accurate your marshmallow launching is.

LICKETY-SPLIT LEPRECHAUN HAT

Top o' the morning to you! Your leprechaun will tip his hat in amazement at this ingenious design.

DIFFICULTY 🍀 🍀 🍀

LEPRECHAUN APPEAL

Leprechauns love a good top hat!

MATERIALS

Paper plates
Scissors*
Green acrylic paint
Hot glue gun*
Craft glue
Tape
Construction paper, green, black, and yellow
Glitter (optional)
Craft sticks or straws for ladder
Sparkly decorations (gemstones, coins, or
    rainbow candies)

STEAM CONNECTION

Mathematics plays a key role in making this trap. Manipulating the paper plate to cut out the center requires calculating the diameter (the length of the line that passes through the center of a shape; i.e., the width of the circle) as well as accurately measuring a green circle to affix on top of your cylinder-shaped hat (another geometric shape). Grab your ruler and determine if you want to measure in inches (American measurement system) or centimeters (metric system). This takes concentration and steady fingers.

1 Take a paper plate and cut out the center. Paint the plate green and let dry. This will be the brim of the paper hat.

Paper plate

8½ x 11 in. green paper

2 Tape or glue two pieces of green construction paper together and form a cylinder—this will be the body of your hat.

↑
Tape

8½ x 11 in. green paper

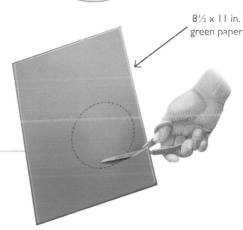

3 Cut out a green circle to affix on top of your hat. Gently fold this green circle in half and cut out a small square in the center. Place the square back over its cutout and tape down one side—this will be your trap door!

2½ x 8½
in. strips

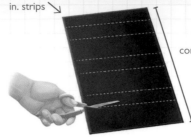

8½ x 11 in.
construction paper

Yellow cutout
(buckle)

Glitter

4 Tape the paper hat brim from step 1 to your green cylinder.

Circle and square cutouts from step 3

Tape

Paper plate from step 1

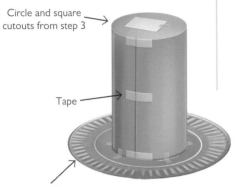

5 Cut out two 2½ x 8 ½ in. strips of black paper and tape them together to form the hatband.

8½ x 11 in.
construction paper

6 Cut out a yellow buckle (a square with a smaller square cut out of the center) from construction paper.

Optional: Spread glue on the buckle and sprinkle with glitter. Let dry, then attach to black hatband.

Two 2½ x 8½
in. strips of
paper

Yellow cutout (buckle)

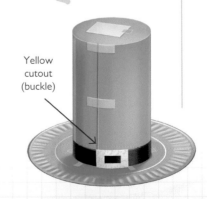

DID YOU KNOW?

The first St. Patrick's Day parade took place in New York City on March 17, 1762. Irish soldiers serving in the English military celebrated their Irish roots with singing, dancing, marching, and music!

7 Create a ladder using craft sticks or straws to attach onto your hat (remember, it has to reach the top). With <u>adult supervision</u>, hot glue sparkly coins or rainbow candies alongside your ladder to bait your leprechaun into climbing.

Note: Attach your hat to a cool base. Either construction paper or a foam board will work great. You can add a fun pathway, signs, and other enticing elements to lure your leprechaun up the ladder!

Candy or gems

MAGIC MUNCH

This crunchy snack is sure to lure your leprechaun and will also serve
as a tasty treat while you work hard constructing your traps!

DIFFICULTY

LEPRECHAUN APPEAL

INGREDIENTS

Plain popcorn, popped*

Pretzels, chopped*

Plain rice cereal squares

Mini marshmallows

White chocolate chips

Rainbow sprinkles

Green-coated milk
    chocolate candies

STEAM CONNECTION

Measuring is key in this activity. But not measuring with
a ruler—we're using a measuring cup. For this recipe, it
is up to you to come up with the measurements—start
with half a cup of each ingredient and experiment with
how different ratios of ingredients make this recipe
sweeter, saltier, or crunchier. There is no wrong combination; just keep in mind that the more ingredients you
add, the more people it will feed!

1. Spread popcorn, pretzels, rice cereal squares, and marsh-mallows on a parchment-lined baking sheet.

2. With <u>adult supervision</u>, use a microwave or double boiler to melt the white chocolate chips. Use a spoon to drizzle the melted choc-olate on top of the snack mix.

3. Scatter the green chocolate candies and sprinkles on top of the white chocolate drizzle.

4. Refrigerate for half an hour to solidify the white chocolate drizzle.

Note: You can substitute peanuts for popcorn, or raisins for marshmallows and make it trail mix style!

MASON O'MALLEY TRAP

Even the lithest of leprechauns can't hold their balance on top of this trap.

DIFFICULTY 🍀 🍀 🍀

LEPRECHAUN APPEAL

MATERIALS

Empty jar, such as a mason jar

Craft paper (wide enough to wrap around jar)

Scissors*

Construction paper, variety of colors

Wooden skewers or craft sticks

Toothpicks

Hot glue gun*

Sparkly gems or coins

STEAM CONNECTION

It's important to carefully measure the diameter of the mason jar mouth on the paper in order to cut out the perfectly sized trap door—if the paper cutout is too big, the trap door won't work, but if it's too small, the trap door will not be a secret! Experiment with just the right width door for your jar.

1 Decorate the craft paper that will go around the jar. Cutting several pieces of paper and wrapping them around the jar works great too. You can add different rows of paper depending on what colorful paper you have. Don't overload the paper with glue though, as the paper needs to remain flexible enough to wrap around the jar.

Mason jar

Tape

Craft paper

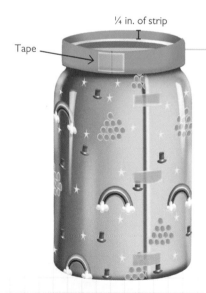

¼ in. of strip

Tape

2 Measure the circumference of the jar's mouth and cut a 2-in. wide strip of paper to this length. Wrap it around the top of the jar, leaving ¼ in. of the strip sticking up around the circumference of the opening. Tape securely.

2-in.-wide strip

8½ x 11 in. construction paper

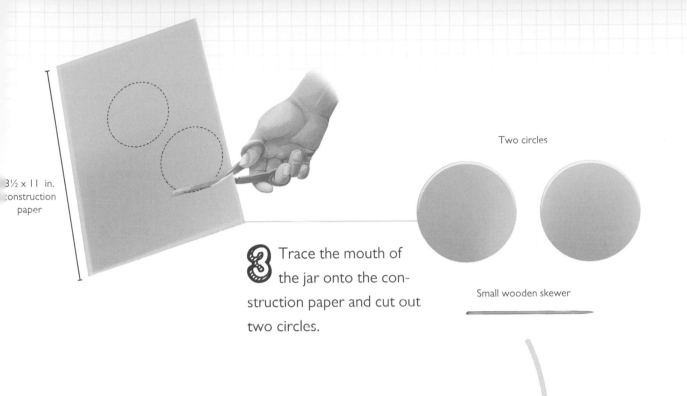

8½ x 11 in. construction paper

Two circles

Small wooden skewer

3 Trace the mouth of the jar onto the construction paper and cut out two circles.

4 Take a small wooden skewer longer than the diameter of the jar and the paper circles and glue it evenly between your two circles like a sandwich. This will be your tricky trap door! Glue some sparkly treasures on top to lure the leprechaun close.

Small wooden skewer

Shiny decorations

Glue skewer to one circle.

Glue other circle on top, so skewer is in between.

Example of sandwich on skewer. Do not attempt.

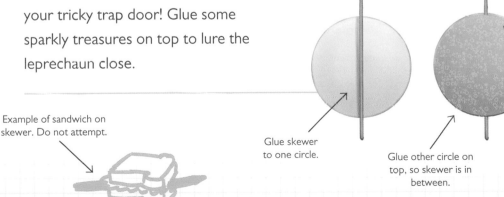

Skewer poked
through paper strip

5 Poke the skewer through the ¼ in. strip of paper that is sticking above mason jar.

Two wooden
skewers

Toothpicks

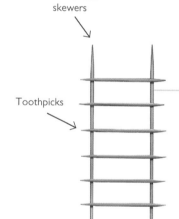

6 Take two long skewers or craft sticks and create a ladder to prop against your trap. Glue the top of ladder against your trap if it won't stay put.

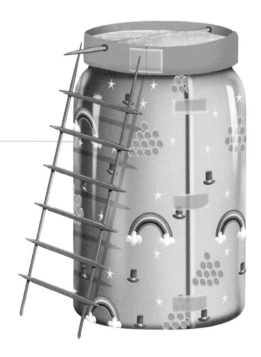

DID YOU KNOW?

||||||||||||||||||||||||||||||||||||||||||||||||||||||||||||||||||||||

The shamrock is Ireland's national symbol and, along with the harp, is a registered trademark of the island!

MARSHMALLOW BRIDGE

Create a marshmallow bridge that can connect two of your
traps together to make one big leprechaun trap!

DIFFICULTY 🍀 🍀

LEPRECHAUN APPEAL

MATERIALS

- 1 bag marshmallows, mini and/or campfire
  size
- 1 box toothpicks

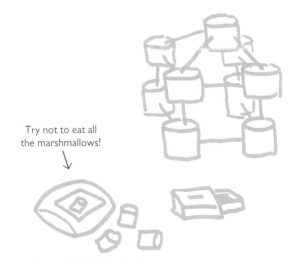

Try not to eat all
the marshmallows!

STEAM CONNECTION

All structures are built to support a certain load.
Some loads are constant (static) and others are
dynamic (change). Engineers have to determine
how to design bridges to withstand dynamic
changes, such as hurricanes and earthquakes,
and static loads, like cars driving and equipment
usage. What will your bridge support? What
combination of toothpicks and marshmallows
make a bridge structurally sound? Triangular
or rectangular design? Mini-marshmallows or
campfire marshmallows?

1 In this activity, experiment with different designs and combinations of toothpicks and marshmallows. As a starting design, make an equilateral triangle—a triangle with three equal sides—out of three toothpicks "glued" together at the ends with three marshmallows.

2 Use the marshmallow at one of the points of this triangle as the starting marshmallow for the corner of a second triangle. Keep the bottoms of the two triangles together in a straight line.

3 Make four connected triangles this way, all with their bottom toothpicks connected in a straight line. Then connect the four top points of the triangles with three toothpicks, one between each point. This will be one side of your bridge.

4 Repeat steps 1–3 to create the second side of your bridge.

5 Now connect the two sides of your bridge! Poke toothpicks at a perpendicular (90°) angle into the marshmallows at each joint of one side of the bridge. Then slowly connect each marshmallow on the other side of the bridge to each corresponding perpendicular toothpick.

6 Test the strength of your bridge by placing it so it spans two tables. If it stays up, test it further by adding a static load, such as placing a toy car on top of it, or a dynamic load, such as putting a fan next to it.

Challenge yourself by trying different designs and different combinations of marshmallows. Perform the same tests to see which design works best under pressure!

LEPRECHAUN RUN

Zig zag zoom! Calling all daredevils! This slide will blow the hat right off your leprechaun!

MATERIALS

Hot glue gun*
Scissors*
Craft glue
Glitter
2–3 cardboard paper
    towel tubes
24 x 36 in. poster or
    foam board
Construction paper
    for signs
Small box
Tissue paper
Marble

DIFFICULTY 🍀 🍀 🍀 🍀

LEPRECHAUN APPEAL

STEAM CONNECTION

This trap will get you experimenting with physics! Marble runs explore the science of conservation of energy. Once the marble is released, its potential energy (stored energy) turns into kinetic energy (energy of motion). This kinetic energy combines with gravity and pulls the marble down the tubes and as it goes down the tube, it accelerates. Alternating the positions of your tubes will change the marble (and leprechaun) speed, so experiment with different angles to find out the quickest way to get your leprechaun to the bottom of the trap!

Paper towel tubes

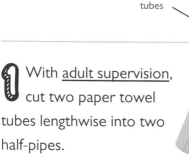

Half-pipe

Glue

Glitter

1 With <u>adult supervision</u>, cut two paper towel tubes lengthwise into two half-pipes.

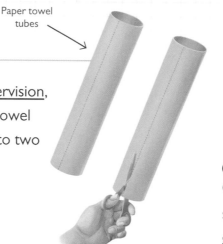

2 Mix craft glue and glitter. Paint the tube segments with the glue and glitter mixture.

Foam board

DID YOU KNOW?

|||||||||||||||||||||||||||||||||||||||||||

Leprechauns aren't the only sprites in European folklore and legends. Holland and the Isle of Man have their own iterations of these small, gnomelike creatures too!

3 With <u>adult supervision</u>, hot glue your half-pipes (open side facing up) in a zigzag formation onto the foam board, with each half-pipe ending 1 in. or so above where the next half-pipe would begin. Let dry. Leave enough room between the end of the last half-pipe and the bottom of the foam board to place your small box at the bottom.

Prior to gluing, position your tubes and have someone hold them in place so you can test your slide with a marble and make sure it lands in the box. Reposition the half-pipes as necessary to create a smooth ride from top to bottom!

Paper towel tube segment

8½ x 11 in. construction paper

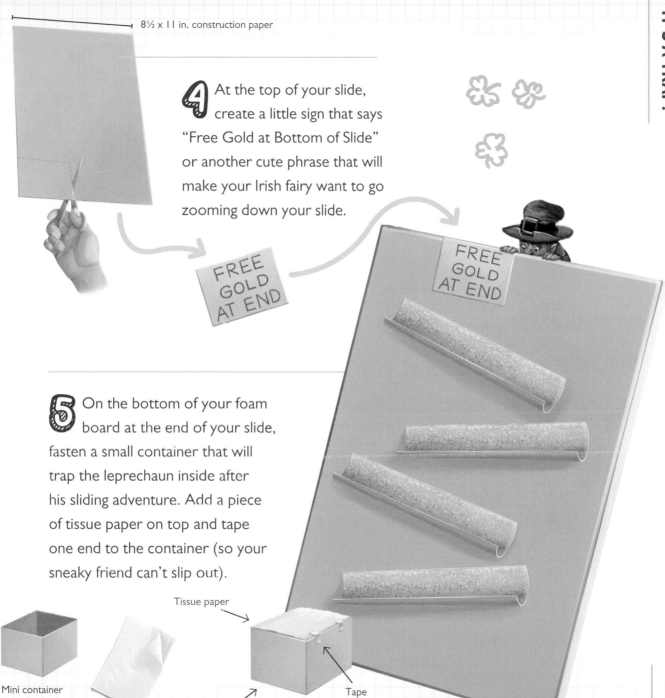

4 At the top of your slide, create a little sign that says "Free Gold at Bottom of Slide" or another cute phrase that will make your Irish fairy want to go zooming down your slide.

FREE GOLD AT END

5 On the bottom of your foam board at the end of your slide, fasten a small container that will trap the leprechaun inside after his sliding adventure. Add a piece of tissue paper on top and tape one end to the container (so your sneaky friend can't slip out).

FREE GOLD AT END

Tissue paper

Mini container

Tissue paper

Mini container

Tape

6 Prop up your foam board against a wall or other flat surface so your slide *zippity zooms* your leprechaun into the trap!

FREE
GOLD
AT END

LEANING LEPRECHAUN TOWER

Add a leaning tower to any trap to make it trickier for your leprechaun to sneak past.

DIFFICULTY 🍀 🍀 🍀

LEPRECHAUN APPEAL

MATERIALS

Small cups, paper or plastic
Wide craft sticks
Small toy blocks

STEAM CONNECTION

Finding the right balance of plastic cups, small blocks, and craft sticks to build the tallest tower requires experimenting with different sized bases and layering the craft sticks accordingly. Can you build a tower with just one cup as a base? What about one block? How can you incorporate your structure into another leprechaun trap?

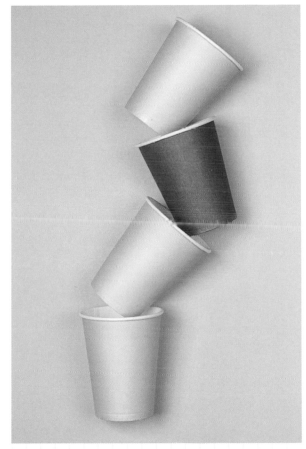

1 Start by placing two cups face down on a flat surface, a few inches apart.

2 Lay one end of a craft stick across the top of one cup and place a toy block on top to hold it in place. The stick should be parallel to the flat surface. If one block is not heavy enough to weigh the stick down, add additional blocks. Repeat for the second cup. The sticks should be parallel to one another.

3 Lay a new craft stick across the other ends of the sticks from step 2 and slowly start stacking cups on top of the stick. To balance the weight of these new cups, add additional blocks on top of the ones from step 2.

4 Experiment with your tower—add more layers of cups and stack more blocks to see what you can create without knocking the tower over. Add more cups to your base to create a huge tower that your leprechaun will be sure to marvel at!

RAINBOW MOTEL

Your little leprechaun is tired from all his shoemaking, trick-playing, and rainbow-spying adventures—let's offer him a place to rest!

DIFFICULTY 🍀 🍀 🍀 🍀

LEPRECHAUN APPEAL

MATERIALS

Scissors*

Interlocking building blocks, such as Legos

Shoebox with lid

Pipe cleaners

Cotton balls

Craft glue

Water

Thick paintbrush

Tissue paper, variety of colors

Small container for mixing materials

Disposable 6-in. ruler or strip of
   cardboard

Stickers, gold coins, or other
   materials for decoration

STEAM CONNECTION

This trap uses a simple machine called the lever. A lever is a rigid bar (in this case, the seesaw) resting on a pivot called a fulcrum. Levers are used to lift heavy loads! The whole purpose of simple machines is to make work easier. What kinds of objects can you set on one end of your seesaw to lure in the leprechaun? Should the load be heavier or lighter than a leprechaun?

1 Create stairs using combinations of Legos. Stairs should reach the roof of the box so your leprechaun can easily walk onto it.

2 Position your shoebox next to the stairs. With <u>adult supervision</u>, cut a small square on top of your shoebox lid toward the rear. (You need to leave room for the seesaw in front!)

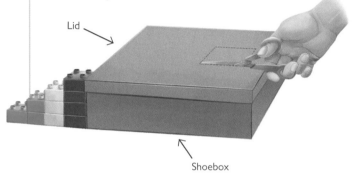

Lid

Shoebox

3 Messy alert! Combine equal parts glue and water to make a sticky mixture. Using a paintbrush, paint sections of your box with the glue mixture, and layer small pieces of tissue paper until your motel is covered. It should look like a parade float! Let dry.

Paper your shoebox lid separately in case you want to add anything INSIDE the box. That way the lid won't be stuck!

Glue   Water

Tissue paper

4 Decorate your ruler with glitter, tissue paper, and stickers—this will be a seesaw to trap your leprechaun later.

Glitter

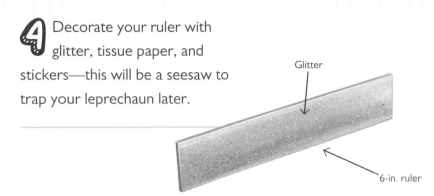

6-in. ruler

5 Take a piece of tissue paper and tape one side over the cutout on the box. Add some gold coins or a little treasure box on the other side of the tissue-paper trap door.

Tissue paper

Tissue paper trap door

Tape

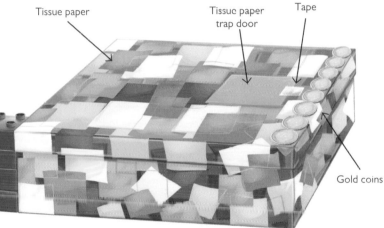

Gold coins

Pipe cleaners

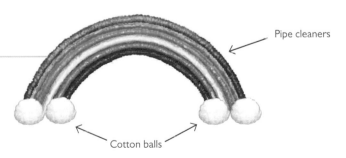

6 Take rainbow pipe cleaners and shape them into a rainbow. Glue cotton balls on the end and fasten it to the top of your motel.

Cotton balls

7 Time to set up! Position your seesaw on top of the motel, using a cotton ball as the fulcrum. When your sneaky Irish lad walks up the stairs, he'll see a seesaw and gold—not realizing that the seesaw hides a trap door into the "motel"!

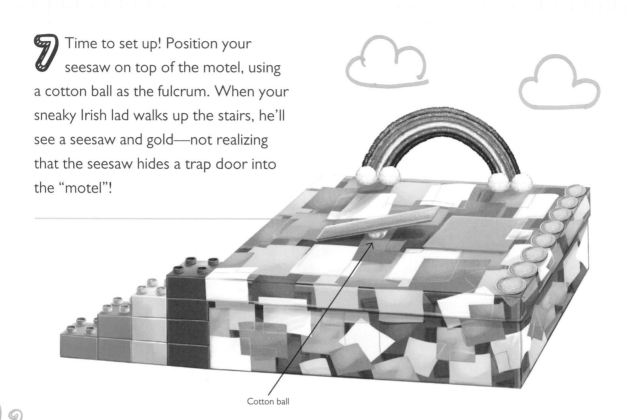

Cotton ball

DID YOU KNOW?

||||||||||||||||||||||||||||||||||||||||||||||||||||||||||||||||||||||||||

There is a nine-thousand-year-old tradition in Ireland of making roofs out of straws, reeds, or heather—a process called "thatching." Only about 1,500 buildings on the island have thatched roofs today, but during the nineteenth century, almost half the houses had this type of roof.

POT O' GOLD SUCCULENTS

Lure your leprechaun into any trap with a little help from these green plants!

DIFFICULTY 🍀 🍀

LEPRECHAUN APPEAL

MATERIALS

6 small pots/planters

Shallow dish or paper plate

Small bag of potting soil

6 tiny succulent plants

Sponge

Gold paint

Paper towels

STEAM CONNECTION

Succulent plants are extra special because they have shallow roots and absorb water more quickly than other plants, which help them survive in the dry heat of the desert. Succulent plants such as cacti, aloes, and agaves survive the lack of water and intense heat by storing plenty of water in their roots, stems, or leaves, which is why they do not need to be watered often. Since succulents can be tricky, keep a log of when you water the plants. After a few months have passed, look back at your log to see if certain seasons require the plants to be watered more frequently than others.

1. Pour gold paint in a shallow dish or paper plate.

2. Place your pots upside down on paper towels.

3. Gently dip the sponge into the paint and dab the pots to cover the surface. Let dry.

4. Once your pots o' gold are dry, flip right side up and fill two-thirds up with potting soil.

5. Make a little hollow for the roots by scooping the potting soil to the side with your fingers.

6. *Gently* press your succulents' roots into the potting soil and pat down soil around them.

Depending on your succulent plant variety and size, they will need around a tablespoon of water about once a week.

TOP O' THE HAT

This clever disguise will lure even the most suspicious Irish fairy.

DIFFICULTY

LEPRECHAUN APPEAL

MATERIALS

Old hat or store-bought St. Patrick's Day hat

Utility knife*

Craft sticks

Hot glue gun*

Craft glue

Multicolored pipe cleaners

Gift bag stuffing or long strands of shredded paper, gold or silver

Glitter

Leprechaun bait, such as gold coins

STEAM CONNECTION

For this trap, you can use geometry to determine the exact center of the hat. If you have a circular hat, place it on a sheet of paper and trace around the bottom border of the rim. Remove the hat and draw a box around the circle you just traced, making sure that each line of the box touches the edge of the circle. Draw two diagonal lines inside the box, and the point at which they intersect is the center of the hat. Position the paper directly on top of the hat and poke a pen through the paper to mark the center.

1 Hot glue your craft sticks together to create a ladder. Add strips of glue onto each rung and sprinkle glitter on top. Let dry.

Six craft sticks

Glitter

2 Carefully cut out a hole on top of your leprechaun hat.

St. Patrick's Day hat

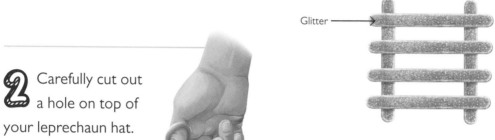

3 Take five pipe cleaners and bend into a rainbow shape.

One red, one orange, one yellow, one green and one blue

DID YOU KNOW?

Ireland's nickname is "the Emerald Isle." Since the island's weather is influenced by the Atlantic Ocean, Ireland receives lots of rain, which creates the country's lush green farmlands and fields.

Small slits in top of
hat, next to the hole

4 With <u>adult supervision</u>, cut two small slits on either side of your hat hole and stick the ends of the pipe-cleaner rainbow into them. Bend the ends around the slits and hat hole so they are securely in place.

Insert ends of pipe
cleaners into slits.

Small pot of gold
or gold coins

Two more pipe
cleaners, any color

Two pipe cleaners
wrapped

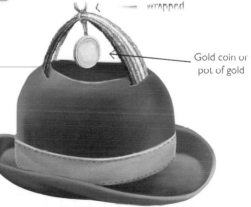

Gold coin or
pot of gold

5 Take two pipe cleaners. Wrap one end around the center of the rainbow, leaving the long end to wrap around your leprechaun bait. If you do not have a little pot, use some gold coins (glued onto the pipe cleaner ends). This bait will dangle above the sneaky hole on top of the hat!

Shredded paper

6 Stuff the hat hole opening with gift bag stuffing or shredded paper.

7 Prop your glittery ladder against your hat and wait for your tricky fellow to follow the pot o' gold!

RAINBOW ICE TUNNELS

Ice blocks and color squirts create a dazzling surprise!

MATERIALS

Different sized plastic containers (small to medium)

Liquid watercolors (or food coloring, but watercolors work best)

Medicine droppers or pipettes, one for each color

Measuring spoons

Small plastic cups to hold paint

Salt

STEAM CONNECTION

This activity uses a similar principle applied to roads during snow and icy weather. Salt is sprinkled on top of snow because salt lowers water's freezing point (the temperature at which a liquid changes to a solid) and prevents the snowy water from refreezing. In this activity, when the saltwater mixture touches the ice, we can see how the ice melts much quicker than it normally would. Inserting the salty mixture on the ice blocks requires different tools—which one penetrates the ice the best?

DIFFICULTY 🍀

LEPRECHAUN APPEAL

1 Freeze water in various containers overnight.

2 When you're ready for the fun, pour several tablespoons of watercolor into plastic cups. Add ½ teaspoon of salt at a time and stir until mixture has thickened but is not chunky.

3 Pop your ice blocks out of the containers and put them on a baking sheet.

4 Fill your droppers with the salt paint and slowly squeeze the liquid onto your ice blocks. The watercolor ice mixture creates colorful tunnels as it melts the ice. Have your camera ready—there will be some beautiful rainbow surprises happening!

LEPRECHAUN LAUNDROMAT

Even the trickiest tricksters need clean clothes and fresh socks.

MATERIALS

Medium size box (shoebox can work too)

Scissors*

2 paint stirrers

Nontoxic acrylic paint

Multicolored construction paper or printed
craft paper for clothes

Thick string

Tape

Clay or putty

Craft sticks

Mini clothespins (optional)

Paper boxes, building blocks, or small
dollhouse furniture (optional)

Craft glue

Black marker

DIFFICULTY 🍀 🍀 🍀 🍀

LEPRECHAUN APPEAL

STEAM CONNECTION

This trap requires critical thinking about weight for
this clothesline as you find out how many clothes
you can hang on the line before it gets too heavy
and falls down. How taut does the line need
to be to hold all the clothes? Are there better
options for clipping our leprechaun lad's bloom-
ers? Engineers, buckle up—being precise and
thoughtful about this tricky trap's main attraction
is a must.

1 Create doors and windows for our Leprechaun Laundromat. Using a black marker, sketch out two doors and several windows around the perimeter of your box (open side up).

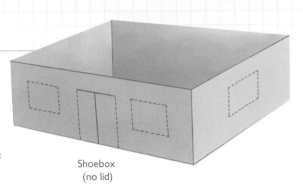

Shoebox
(no lid)

2 With <u>adult supervision</u>, carefully cut out your doors and windows, but have your door hinge attached at the TOP (not the side). This will be propped open with a stick to snag your sneaky lad later on.

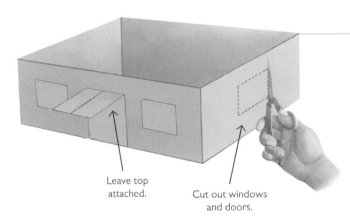

Leave top
attached.

Cut out windows
and doors.

3 Paint the outside of your box in gold, green, and white. Paint the bottom brown and let dry.

After the paint has dried, you might want to add some cute painted window shutters, gold doorknobs, and other details to make your trap stand out.

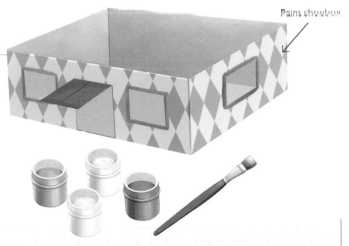

Paint shoebox

Paint

67

Craft sticks

Building blocks

Strips of construction paper

Inside of shoebox

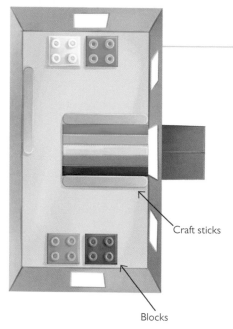

Craft sticks

Blocks

Paper towel roll

4 Once your box is dry, it's time to decorate the bottom! Be sure to add a rainbow path down the center of your Laundromat. Create little mini washers and dryers, either out of building blocks or paper and craft sticks, to go alongside the path.

Mini washers and dryers can be made out of paper boxes, building blocks, or dollhouse furniture. Be creative with this step and use what you have around the house!

5 Take two paper towel tubes (or paint stirrers) and glue them on opposite sides of your box, across from each other. Make sure they are sticking up at least 1 in. from the edge of the box. They will be the posts for your laundry line.

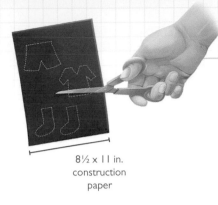

8½ x 11 in.
construction
paper

6 Draw and cut out little leprechaun clothes that will hang on your laundry line…knickers, shirts, long green socks, coat (with shiny buttons, of course), and more.

Clothes   String   Tape

7 Tape a piece of yarn or thick string to the top of each paper towel tube or stirrer. Make sure it is securely fastened and won't fall once the laundry is attached!

8 Carefully attach your clothes to the laundry line using tape or hot glue. (Some craft stores and dollar bin sections have mini clothespins.)

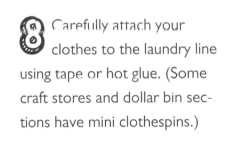

69

Small pieces of paper

Craft sticks

9 A sign is a must! Create little signs attached to craft sticks. Stand them up with clay or some sort of putty (as in the Shamrock Diner). Phrases like "Get a new coat!" or "Fresh shirts for leprechaun lads!" will draw your leprechaun in for some freshly pressed clothes.

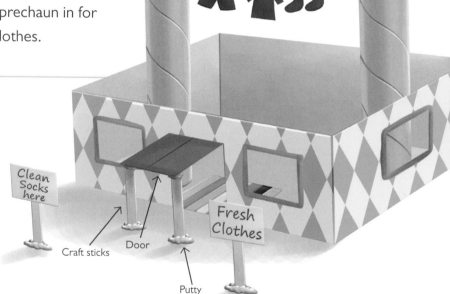

Clean Socks here

Fresh Clothes

← Modeling clay or putty

10 Prop open your door with a craft stick. Attach teeny balls of putty to the top and bottom of the stick to secure it in place before your leprechaun knocks it over!

Clean Socks here

Fresh Clothes

Craft sticks

Door

Putty

DID YOU KNOW?

An Irishman helped redesign the White House! Architect James Hoban was raised in County Kilkenny but immigrated to the United States in 1785. After the original White House burned down in 1814, Hoban was brought on to assist in restoring the building.

THE SNIP-SNAP LEPRECHAUN TRAP 2000

Your greedy cobbler can't resist this pile of gold—he'll be caught in a quick *snip-snap*!

DIFFICULTY

LEPRECHAUN APPEAL

STEAM CONNECTION

This trap incorporates physics and mechanics as we discover the appropriate weight for pebbles to secure the string. In addition, gravity is a force of motion. Once the leprechaun knocks over the pebbles securing the string, gravity pulls down the trap to fall on top of him! Is there something you could construct to keep your cup from being too heavy for the string...but durable enough so your leprechaun cannot sneak out? Agile fingers need to thread the string through the cup and ensure it is centered above the tempting treasures for your leprechaun.

MATERIALS

Shoebox (no lid)

Nontoxic acrylic paint

Gold paint for gold nuggets

Poking tool* (screwdriver works great)

Small cup, paper or plastic

Thick string or yarn

White clay

Construction paper, variety of colors

Rainbow candies (optional, for decoration)

Paintbrush

Scissors*

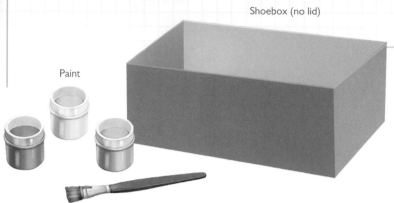

Shoebox (no lid)

Paint

1 Paint the inside and outside of the shoebox in St. Patrick's Day colors. Let dry.

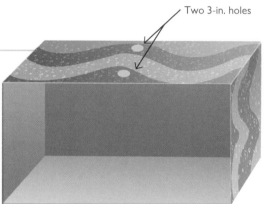

Two 3-in. holes

Box on side with opening facing out

2 Turn shoebox on its small side, with opening sideways. Poke a large hole (about the size of a pencil eraser) on the top of the shoebox toward the front edge. Using that hole as your guide, measure 3 in. behind that hole and poke another hole (same size) there. This will be where you thread your cup string through.

String

Paper cup

3 Poke a hole through the bottom of the small cup and thread string through it, knotting the end (inside the cup) until the string/yarn cannot pull through.

Knot

Hole in bottom of cup

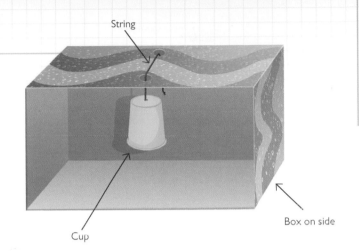

String

Box on side

Cup

4 Take the remaining string and thread it upward through the first box hole, then downward through the second box hole. The leftover string will be in the trap and weighed down by a gold nugget.

White modeling clay

Little nuggets

Paint nuggets gold.

5 Form white clay into small nuggets. Paint gold.

6 Take several gold nuggets and place them under the dangling cup, and on TOP of the excess string. The stickiness of the clay should keep the string secure—until your leprechaun lad tries to grab it, of course! Once the string is let loose, *snap!* Your leprechaun will be trapped.

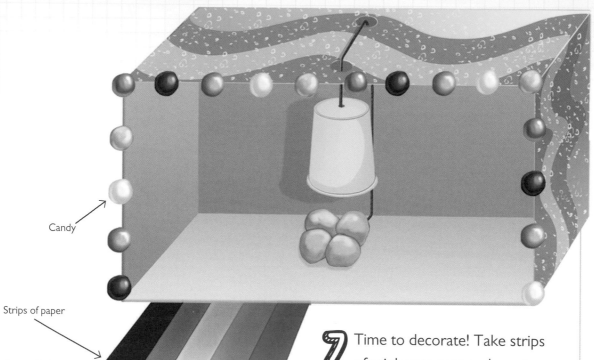

Candy

Strips of paper

Cotton balls

7 Time to decorate! Take strips of rainbow paper and create a rainbow path to your trap. Glue rainbow-colored candies around the outside rim of your shoebox.

Cut strips from each piece of colored paper.

Construction paper

DID YOU KNOW?

||||||||||||||||||||||||||||||||||||||||||||||||||||||||||

Under European law, leprechauns are listed as an endangered species. There is an official safe haven in Carlingford, Ireland, for leprechauns to hide in.

Rainbow-colored candy

Cotton balls

MINI IRISH TERRARIUM

Grow a miniature Irish garden that will stop a leprechaun right in his tracks!

DIFFICULTY 🍀 🍀 🍀

LEPRECHAUN APPEAL

MATERIALS

Mason jar with lid (preferably with removable
    lid disk insert)
1 cup sand
1 cup tiny rocks or pebbles (often called pea
    gravel)
1 cup potting soil
1 sheet card stock
1 packet clover seeds
Pencil
Tablespoon
Decorations

*Decorations add a cute touch to your terrarium, but
they have to be tiny and can get wet and humid. Little
ceramic bunnies, fairies, or flowers will make your
garden feel like a little piece of Ireland in a jar. You
can also form tiny creatures or Irish cottages for your
terrarium using oven-bake clay.*

STEAM CONNECTION

This activity will show you the water cycle in
action! After you water your terrarium, the water
evaporates and droplets collect at the top of your
terrarium. These droplets then drip down to
nourish your plants like rain. Your garden recycles
the water you provide, over and over again, which
is why you only need to water them every few
weeks. Be sure to look up additional information
on terrarium care based on the types of plants
you have and the specific conditions your plants
may need. Keep track of growth and watering in a
science log to determine how often you need to
replenish the water in your own ecosystem.

1 Layer! Start with 1 in. of pebbles on the bottom of a clean mason jar.

2 Now add 1 in. of sand.

3 Add 1 ½ in. (approximately) of potting soil on top of the sand. Carefully use the tip of your pencil eraser to poke the soil, creating tiny little holes.

4 Sprinkle your grass or clover seed over the potting soil and dust the seeds with a tablespoon of potting soil.

5 Add decorations gently on the soil layer.

6 Sprinkle a tablespoon of water onto the dirt.

7 Take your mason jar lid (round disk) and trace its shape on your card stock. Cut this circle out and secure it onto your mason jar with the band.

8 Poke a few holes into the paper so your seeds can get air!

Water your seeds every other day with a tablespoon of water. If you start to notice mold in your jar, take the top off and let it get more air for a few days.

LUCK O' THE IRISH WISHING WELL

Get ready to make your three wishes! Your leprechaun won't be able to resist this fancy-looking wishing well.

DIFFICULTY

LEPRECHAUN APPEAL

MATERIALS

Recycled cardboard milk carton

Nontoxic acrylic paint

Sponge cut into small rectangles

2 paint stirrers

Hot glue gun*

Pencil

Thick string or yarn, 12 in.

Building blocks

Mini pot of gold or other dangling treasure that isn't heavy

STEAM CONNECTION

This trap involves another simple machine from our physics notebook—the pulley! A pulley uses a wheel (in this case, a pencil) and a rope to hold up the leprechaun bait. What happens if the bait is heavier? Would a thicker pencil work better? Or another long, round instrument? Experiment with different weights of your leprechaun bait to see how well your rope will hold it. Is there a way to attach a handle to your pencil so you can pull the leprechaun bait up and down?

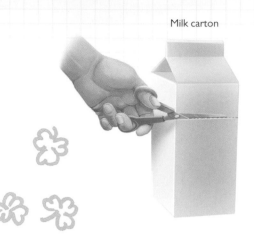

Milk carton

1 With <u>adult supervision</u>, take your milk carton and cut the top off, two thirds up from the bottom.

2 Take your sponges and dip them into brown, gray, and black paint—create a brick-like design on the outside of your milk carton. Let dry.

Sponge cut into smaller pieces

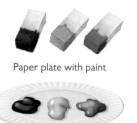

Paper plate with paint

Milk carton stamped with brick pattern

DID YOU KNOW?

According to Irish legend, the four leaves on the four-leaf clover represent hope, faith, love, and luck. It is estimated that there are ten thousand three-leaf clovers for every ONE four-leaf clover—hence you are very lucky if you find one!

With <u>adult supervision</u>, hot glue paint stirrers opposite one another on the inside *bottom* half of your carton. The tops of the paint stirrers should stick up several inches (the top half of your carton will be attached to them later on).

Bottom half of carton

Two paint stirrers

Top half of carton

Pencil

½ in.

Take the top half of your milk carton and measure ½ in. above the bottom. Make a pencil mark to remember your measurement. Carefully poke a pencil at the pencil mark from one end through your carton, and out the other (leave the pencil centered in the well).

Be patient with this step—steady fingers! Take the yarn or string and tape one end to the middle of the pencil inside the carton. Wrap around several times until just ½ in. is left to wrap around your pot of gold. Make sure the string is secure so it won't get weighed down by your pot of gold.

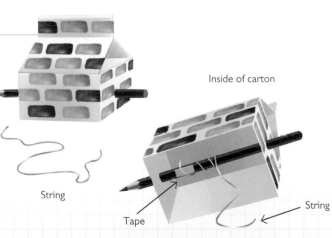

Inside of carton

String

Tape

String

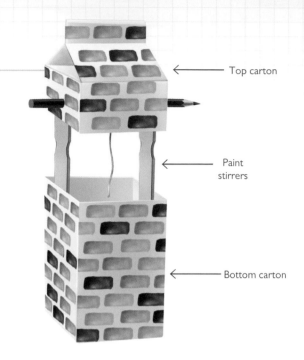

Top carton

Paint stirrers

Bottom carton

6 Spread hot glue on 1 in. of the *outside* of your paint stirrers. Attach the top half of your milk carton to the stirrer sticks, leaving approximately 2 in. in between. Remember, this is a wishing well, so you will need space in between the bottom and top halves of your milk carton. Make sure the top piece is set.

7 Create stairs out of building blocks to lead up to the wishing well and dangling pot of gold! Make some creative signs that will catch your leprechaun's eye, such as "Wishing Well ahead!"

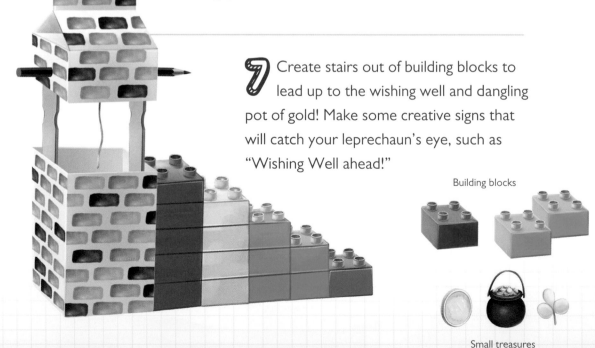

Building blocks

Small treasures

8 Attach your mini pot of gold or other treasure to the end of your string. It can't be heavy or it will pull down your string and fall into the well (remember, this is what we want the leprechaun to do!). Experiment with what works best to keep your treasure dangling.

CASTLES IN IRELAND

Calling all architects! Can you create a castle like the ones found
along the breathtaking landscape of the Emerald Isle?

DIFFICULTY

LEPRECHAUN APPEAL

MATERIALS

- Favorite set of building blocks
- Computer or tablet* or books about Irish
  castles
- Printer and computer paper (optional)

STEAM CONNECTION

This bonus activity requires technology and
engineering skills to determine which materials
can be used to construct a castle in the most
structurally sound, appropriate, and realistic-
looking way. Castles have tons of nooks and
crannies—how can you replicate those? What
did Irish folk do to stabilize and secure the
materials to create this timeless architecture?
Tech-savvy kids could attempt recreating the
castles in Minecraft!

1 Search for pictures of castles in Ireland.

2 Ask a grown-up to print out a favorite
picture (optional).

3 Use this picture for inspiration as you
construct your own Irish castle using
your building blocks. Is there a way you can
incorporate this block castle into one of your
tricky traps?

MAKE YOUR OWN LEPRECHAUN-TRAPPING KIT

Put your own creative skills to the test and create your very own leprechaun trap!

SUGGESTED MATERIALS

How to Catch a Leprechaun by Adam Wallace

Pencil and notepad

Construction paper

Glue

Tape

Shoebox

Paint and paintbrush

String

Pipe cleaners

Paper towel tubes

Craft sticks

Twist ties

Irish Spring soap (Leprechauns will be drawn to this fresh scent!)

Marshmallow cereal

Gold coins (real or chocolate!)

Basket for all your materials

DIFFICULTY 🍀 🍀 🍀 🍀 🍀

LEPRECHAUN APPEAL

USE YOUR IMAGINATION!

Implement ideas from the traps described in this book and create your own!

1

_____
_____
_____
_____
_____

2

_____
_____
_____
_____
_____

3

_____
_____
_____
_____
_____

4

_____
_____
_____
_____

5

_____
_____
_____
_____
_____

6
_____
_____
_____
_____
_____

7
_____
_____
_____
_____
_____